To Debbie Kovacs, writer, friend to many—including Eva and me.

And, of course, to Eva

—J.B.M.

For Avery and Quinn Garcia Wilson —C.H.

Readers
to **Eaters**

READERS to EATERS
1620 Broadway, Suite 6, San Francisco, CA 94109
readerstoeaters.com

Distributed by Publishers Group West
Printed in the USA by Worzalla, Stevens Point, WI (2/24)

Book design by Christy Hale
Book production by The Kids at Our House
Special thanks to Kevin Daugherty, Education Director, Illinois Farm Bureau Agriculture in the Classroom

The text is set in Clarendon
The art is created using collage, print, and line

10 9 8 7 6 5 4 3 2 1
First Edition

Library of Congress Control Number: 2023914913
ISBN: 978-0-998047775

FARMER EVA'S
GREEN GARDEN LIFE

written by Jacqueline Briggs Martin

illustrated by Christy Hale

Afterword by Eva Sommaripa

Readers
to Eaters

San Francisco, California

My friend Eva Sommaripa lives
so close to the ocean
she can smell the sea,
so close to woods
she can talk to trees.

She farms one field in Massachusetts.
From that small patch, she has grown
a big green garden life
of family, friends, neighbors,
creatures that crawl, fly, squawk, slither,
even microbes too tiny to see,
and so many plants.

Eva never planned to be a farmer.
But one morning at a small market,
she saw bunches of fresh tarragon
and boxes of strawberries.

The strawberries were so red,
the tarragon so green and sweet-smelling,
Eva knew right then she wanted to grow
her own herbs.

Eva dug and hoed and planted.
She watched, watered, and picked off bugs,
and soon she had
parsley for potatoes,
dill for crunchy pickles,
and basil for tomato sandwiches.

Tending plants under the blue sky,
soil on her hands, birdsong all around,
Eva's best good time.
Food, farming, and nature filled her world.

dill

basil

parsley

After a few summers,
Eva was growing more herbs
than her family could eat.
What to do?

She loaded her car with so much green,
trot trotted to Boston and offered
it all to restaurant chefs.

"Try this!" she said to the chefs.
"Delicious!" they said. "Bring us more."

TRY THIS!

pea shoots   sorrel   purple shiso

Eva added pea shoots, sorrel, and purple shiso.
More chefs said,

BRING US
MORE!

Days on Eva's farm were busy
with planting, snipping, sorting, packing.

But work stopped
while the farm team inspected
a praying mantis

or admired a hawk
circling overhead.

At lunchtime, they seasoned
their sandwiches with herbs,
seasoned their talk with laughter.

In the middle of the farm busyness
Eva began to wonder—
what was really going on
under her garden boots?

She read about soil,
talked with soil scientists,
learned of all the helpful critters—
earthworms, centipedes, pillbugs—
and the microbes—too tiny for us to see—
that live in the BROWN UNDERGROUND.

Eva learned that the critters in the soil
eat decaying plant parts and poop out plant food.
And the microbes partner with the plants, too.
Here's how that works:
Eva's plants use sunshine and water
to make the sugars they need to grow.

The sugars that plants don't use
come out through their roots.
Microbes feast on those sugars (and each other),
and they help plant roots
get more nutrients from the soil.
It's an EAT-AROUND-UNDERGROUND-CAFE

Eva adds to the cafe menu:
soil chow chow (compost) made of leaves and weeds,
coffee chaff from her friends at the roastery,
plate-scrapings (no meat) from schools and restaurants.

PLATE
SCRAPINGS

COFFEE
CHAFF

SOIL
CHOW CHOW

Eva even makes "fish and chips" compost
from seaweed and shells.
She's always experimenting with new items
for the compost buffet.

FISH AND
CHIPS

YUM!

EARTHWORM

MICROBES

PILLBUG

CENTIPEDE

The brown underground has made Eva a farming hero.
Eaters and chefs know she grows greens and herbs that
turn salads into adventures of sour, sweet, and crunch,
and flowers that make any table a party table.

Kids and young farmers come from all over
to see the farm and learn from the green garden team.

And, Eva's farm is also home to small wonders.

She grows flowers for pollinators
such as butterflies and bees.

She walks carefully
around nesting killdeer

and garden toads.

One year on a warm, wet spring night
Eva organized a salamander brigade
to carry migrating crawlers
across the busy road next to her farm, to help them
go from their forest home to the pond to lay eggs.

Since then, Eva and the brigade
have saved hundreds of salamanders

Every year, when Eva wants to celebrate
the whole bustling, buzzing green garden life,
she invites friends to a
Longest Day Summer Potluck.

Monica will bake pizza in Eva's outdoor oven,
Geoff will share black garlic spread.
Farm manager Honey Bee will bring
spicy nasturtiums to scatter on salads.

Some will bring pie, some sandwiches.
Eva will make pink sorrel lemonade. "Try this!"
All will eat, laugh, and talk under the summer moon.

And the next day, our friend Eva
will be back living her green garden life—
digging in the brown underground,
watching for small wonders
on her special patch
between the sea and the trees.

A Note from Eva Sommaripa

Dear Reader, Eater, and maybe Future Farmer,

Did this book start you thinking about the communities that are underground—and maybe under your feet right now?

What seems like just dirt and stones is a whole other universe of living creatures. Some we can see but most are only visible with a microscope. For millions of years, the underground communities have turned plants, animals, rocks, and more into soil. The soil produces plants that feed us and other animals. When you eat your favorite foods, remember that all of the ingredients started with the world underground!

Discovery and mystery come with growing food. New kinds of plants show up. So do parts of familiar plants that I hadn't noticed before. Foods I didn't like turn out to be delicious when prepared by a chef who buys what we grow.

At my farm, we work with this underground world to grow food—along with sunshine, rain, and amazing tools. Helping on someone else's farm or garden is a good start.

Photo credit: Michael Piazza

We also gather wild food from the woods, fields, and beaches. These could be berries, leaves, flowers, roots, or mushrooms. Forager groups often welcome new learners.

When you walk on the ground, even in the city, just know that there is a lot going on beneath your feet. You are never alone.

Grow on!

Eva

Eva Sommaripa
Farmer and Owner, Eva's Garden

Eva and the Green Garden Farm: A Woman Farmer

Eva's farm began as a small patch of herbs in 1972. From her three acres, she now grows and sells truckloads of greens, flowers, and herbs (more than 200 kinds) to restaurants, grocery stores, and neighbors—even an ice cream shop.

Eva is the sole owner of her farm and several acres of adjoining forest. According to the United States Department of Agriculture's 2017 Census of Agriculture, nine percent of farms in the United States are owned entirely by women. In addition, women make up 36 percent of the people who operate farms, either by themselves or with partners (but do not necessarily own them). Women crop farmers tend to:

- work on smaller parcels of land than men farmers;
- live on the farms they work;
- grow diverse crops—often vegetables, herbs, and fruits rather than commodity crops like cotton, wheat, or soybeans;
- develop networks to help each other;
- be younger and more likely to be beginning producers, making up over 40% of all new farmers.

In 2014, Eva became the first farmer to receive Wellesley College's prestigious Alumnae Achievement Award. Eva's Garden is such an important place for so many kinds of creatures and has such a rich history that a land preservation group purchased development rights in 2020 for Eva's property, so it will always be protected as a working farm and forest.

Eating Herbs with Eva

Herbs can add flavor and fragrance to our foods. Try some of Eva's favorite ways to eat fresh herbs in your everyday meals. Can you taste the difference?

1. Add chopped fresh herbs such as parsley, basil, dill, or thyme to softened butter or cream cheese. Spread on crackers or toast.

2. Add herbs to salads or sandwiches.

3. Sprinkle chopped fresh herbs on top of a cooked pizza before you eat it. Yum!

4. Make herb tea: add parsley, dill, cilantro, basil or chives (or any combination of these herbs) in water that you have boiled and let steep overnight. You'll have a delicious tea that you can drink by itself or use to make a soup.

Eva's Recipe for Growing Pea Shoots

Pea shoots are fun to grow. They are tasty and they grow very fast.

What you need:

Seeds. Many seed companies sell pea seeds, or if you find dried peas in your grocery store, you can use them.

Soil. Use your own good garden soil or any potting soil from a garden or plant store. If you have compost, mix compost into your soil—about half compost, half soil.

A pot. Your container should be at least three inches deep. You can use a plant pot, a tin can with drainage holes, old baskets—even tipped over straw hats!

What you do:

1. Find an adult to work with you.

2. Soak your pea seeds in water for 24 hours before planting.

3. Put potting soil in your container. Leave an inch of empty space at the top. Gently press down on the soil with your hand.

4. Place your pea seeds on top of the soil. Leave ¼ inch of space around each seed. Cover with about ½ inch of soil.

5. Water gently so you don't flood the soil. Water until the soil feels moist but not slurpy and muddy.

6. Place outside if the weather is mild, or in a sunny window.

7. Check your pea shoots every day. Keep the soil moist to your touch, but not muddy.

8. You can cut your pea shoots as soon as you see leaves, but you will have a bigger crop if you wait until they are about three to five inches tall. If you cut about half-way down the stem, they may grow back and give you another crop.

9. Enjoy your pea shoots in sandwiches, salads, omelets. Share with friends!

Eva's Brown Underground: Eat-around Underground Cafe and Cast of Critters

Eva's plants are sugar factories. They make sugar from carbon dioxide, water, and sunshine. But they make more than they can use. They push out extra sugars through their roots. Microbes (microscopic one-celled organisms) gather around the roots to eat these sugars. But they don't just take from the plant roots, they give back.

Microbes are all around us, in the air, in the soil, on the plants we eat. There are also microbes in our stomachs that help us digest food. Here are some microbes in the soil that help plants digest food:

Bacteria recycle decaying plant material in the soil into nutrients needed by living plant roots. They also help plants absorb more nitrogen and other nutrients. There may be up to one billion bacteria in a teaspoon of soil.

Fungi often look like long threads (called hyphae, hi-fay) under a microscope. These threads can be many yards long. They can detect the presence of plant sugars in the soil and grow to connect to plant roots and digest the sugars made by plants. They are so tiny, and can be so long, they can reach water and nutrients to share with plants that roots can't reach. These fungi are called mycorrhizal fungi.

Protozoa eat organic matter, bacteria, other protozoa, and sometimes fungi. When they eat bacteria, which are rich in nitrogen, they help release the nitrogen into the soil for plants to absorb.

Eva's brown underground and compost piles are also bustling with creatures big enough to see:

Nightcrawler worms breathe through their skin and need to stay moist to survive. They eat decaying plant material.

Red wigglers are smaller than nightcrawlers, and live near the surface of the compost pile. They eat voraciously from the compost—leaves, decaying plant parts, soil and tiny microbes.

Earthworms live deeper in the compost pile than red wigglers. They are also big eaters. Their castings (poops) add nutrients to the soil.

Centipedes are night hunters that live near the surface of the compost. They eat worms and insects.

Millipedes move slowly through the earth or compost on their many legs. They eat  decaying plant material.

Pill bugs and sowbugs are not actually bugs. They are more related to crayfish and shrimp than insects. They have hard shells and segmented bodies. They live in moist dark soil or compost, and eat decaying plant material.

Farmers like Eva and many scientists recognize that the underground cafeteria is the place where all partners are important to the survival of all.

Author's Note

I have loved the work of writing this story about my friend Eva Sommaripa. We are alike in so many ways, it seems as if we have been friends since childhood. Eva is a farmer. I grew up on a farm with a barn full of cows and a garden full of greens and beans, peas and beets.

Eva loves the flavors of fresh food. When I was a child growing up on a dairy farm, fresh garden food was a holiday celebration. My mother was a wonderful cook. She made strawberry shortcake in strawberry season and we thought we were eating like kings and queens. Because there were cows to be milked two times each day, we did not take vacations. But we had good times with garden peas and new potatoes, summer sweet corn with butter and salt, and suppers of crackers and fresh milk. Eva is all about building community by sharing food. I think of her when I share bread with our neighbors, or ripe tomatoes at the local food pantry.

Eva takes much joy in the natural world of her farm and reminds others to look for that joy. She makes me want to share the fun of food and of the outdoors, notice all the small wonders. I hope she will do that for you, too.

Jacqueline Briggs Martin's many books include *Snowflake Bentley*, winner of the Caldecott medal. Farmer Eva is part of her "Food Heroes" series, which include *Farmer Will Allen and the Growing Table*, *Alice Waters and the Trip to Delicious*—and co-written with June Jo Lee—*Chef Roy Choi and the Street Food Remix* and *Sandor Katz and the Tiny Wild*. Jacqueline grew up on a dairy farm in Maine and now lives in Mount Vernon, Iowa. jacquelinebriggsmartin.com.

Christy Hale has illustrated numerous children's books, including *Our School Garden*, published by Readers to Eaters. She is also the author and illustrator of many books, most recently *Copycat: Nature-Inspired Design Around the World*, *Water Land: Land and Water Forms Around the World* and *Dreaming Up: A Celebration of Building*. She lives in Palo Alto, California. christyhale.com.

Eva Sommaripa is a pioneering farmer who started Eva's Garden more than 50 years ago in South Dartmouth, Massachusetts. She has introduced culinary herbs, greens, flowers, and wild foraged goods to Boston area chefs and eaters. In 2014, she became the first farmer to receive Wellesley College's prestigious Alumnae Achievement Award. Eva and her farm is the subject of the book, *Wild Flavors*, written by chef Didi Emmons.

Resources

Personal Interviews and Garden Tour

Farm visits with Eva: April 23, 2019, February 24, 2020.

Phone and online interviews with Eva in 2021, 2022, and 2023.

Phone interview with neighbor Deborah Kovacs, March 22, 2021.

Selected Internet resources

Emmons, Didi. *Wild Flavors: One Chef's Transformative Year Cooking from Eva's Farm.* White River Junction, VT: Chelsea Green, 2011.

Montgomery, David R. & Bikle, Anne. *The Hidden Half of Nature.* New York: W.W. Norton, 2016.

Wolfe, David W. *Tales from the Underground. A Natural History of Subterranean Life.* New York: Basic Books, 2001.

Selected Print resources

Eva's Garden: http://www.evasgreengarden.com

Eva's acceptance speech, Wellesley College Alumnae Achievement Award, March 3, 2014. https://www.youtube.com/watch?v=t-l_EIwksn0

"The Full Conversation: Eva Sommaripa." Blue View Productions. December 16, 2021. https://www.youtube.com/watch?v=ASbrX2T08XE&ab_channel=BlueViewProductions

Hilsman, Angie. "Influential farmer to be recognized for community involvement." *Dartmouth Week*, May 1, 2017. https://dartmouth.theweektoday.com/article/influential-farmer-be-recognized-community-involvement/28234

Tucker, Aimee. "In the Garden of Eva." *NewEngland.com*. August 26, 2013. https://newengland.com/yankee-magazine/food/commercial-herb-garden/

Soil Bacteria and Fungi

Chadwick, Douglas. "Why are Mycorrhizae Important?" *Mother Earth News*. Aug/Sept 2014. https://www.motherearthnews.com/organic-gardening/gardening-techniques/mycorrhizal-fungi-zm0z14aszkin/

Edmonds, Mary, and Natalia Pinzón, "How to Create a Soil Community." Rodale Institute. December 12, 2012. https://rodaleinstitute.org/science/articles/how-to-create-a-soil-community/

Women in Farming

"Honoring Female Farmers and Ranchers this Women's History Month." U.S. Department of Agriculture. March 15, 2023. https://www.usda.gov/media/blog/2023/03/15/honoring-female-farmers-and-ranchers-womens-history-month

Helmer, Jodi. "How Women Farmers are Changing U.S. Agriculture" *Civil Eats*. July 7, 2016. https://civileats.com/2016/07/07/how-women-farmers-are-changing-u-s-agriculture/

Eva with farm manager Honey Bee